THE MYSTERY OF PRAISE

"But thou art holy, O thou that inhabitest the praises of Israel."

Psalm 22:3

By
Franklin N. Abazie

The Mystery of Praise

COPYRIGHT 2018 BY Franklin N Abazie
ISBN: 978:1-945-13-334-3
All right reserved. This book or any portion thereof may not be reproduced or used in any manner whatsoever without the express written permission of the publisher, except for the use of brief quotations in a book review. All Bible quotes are from King James Version and others as noted.

Published by: F N ABAZIE PUBLISHING HOUSE---
a.k.a,
Empowerment Bookstore:

That I may publish with the voice of thanksgiving and tell of all thy wondrous works. **Psalms26:7**

To order additional copies, wholesales or booking: Call the Church office (973-372-7518)
or Empowerment Bookstore Hotline 973-393-8518
Worship address:
343 Sanford Avenue Newark New Jersey 07106
Administrative Head Office address:
33 Schley Street Newark New Jersey 07112
Email:pastorfranknto@yahoo.com
Website www.fnabaziehealingministries.org
Publishing House: www.fnabaziepublishinghouse.org

This book is a production of F N Abazie Publishing House.

A publication Arms of Miracle of God Ministries 2018
First Edition

CONTENTS

THE MANDATE OF THE COMMISSION...........iv

ARMS OF THE COMMISSION............................v

INTRODUCTION..viii

CHAPTER 1

1. The Power of Praise 43

CHAPTER 2

2. Hindrances of Praise 55

CHAPTER 3

3. Prayer of Salvation..74

CHAPTER 4

4. About the Author...83

THE MANDATE OF THE COMMISSION

"THE MOMENT IS DUE TO IMPACT YOUR WORLD THROUGH THE REVIVAL OF THE HEALING & MIRACLE MINISTRY OF JESUS CHRIST OF NAZARETH.

I AM SENDING YOU TO RESTORE HEALTH UNTO THEE AND I WILL HEAL THEE OF THY WOUNDS, SAID THE LORD OF HOST."

ARMS OF THE COMMISSION

1) F N Abazie Ministries-Miracle of God Ministries (Miracle Chapel Intl)

2) F N Abazie TV Ministries: Global Television Ministry Outreach.

3) F N Abazie Radio Ministries: Radio Broadcasting Outreach.

4) F N Abazie Publishing House: Book Publication.

5) F N Abazie Bible School: also called Word of Healing Bible School (W.O.H.B.S)

6) F N Abazie Evangelistic Ass: Miracle of God Ministries: Global Crusade

7) Empowerment Bookstore: Book distribution.

8) F N Abazie Helping Hands: Meeting the help of the needy world wide

9) F N Abazie Disaster Recovery Mission: Global Disaster Recovery.

10) F N Abazie Prison Ministry: Prison Ministry for all convicts "Second chance"

Some of our ministry arms are waiting the appointed time to commence

FAVOR CONFESSION

Father thank you for making me righteous and accepted through the blood of Jesus Christ. Because of that, I am blessed and highly favored by God. I am the subject of your affection. Your favor surrounds me as a shield, and the first thing that people see around me is your favored shield.

Thank you that I have favor with you and man today. All day long people go out of their way to bless me and help me. I have favor with everyone that I deal with today. Doors that were once closed are now opened for me. I receive preferential treatment, and I have special privileges, I am Gods favored child.

No good thing will he withhold from me. Because of Gods favor my enemies cannot triumph over my life. I have supernatural increase and promotion. I declare restoration to everything that the devil has stolen from my life. I have honor in the midst of my adversaries and an increase in assets, especially in real estate and expansion of territories.

Because I am highly favored by God, I experience great victories, supernatural turnarounds, and miraculous breakthrough in the midst of great impossibilities. I receive recognition, prominence, and honor. Petitions are granted to me even by ungodly authorities. Policies, rules, regulations, and laws are changed and reverse on my behalf.

I win battles that I don't even have to fight, because God fights them for me. This is the day, the set time and the designated moment for me to experience the free favor of God, that profusely and lavishly abound on my behalf in Jesus name. Amen.

INTRODUCTION

"And I, if I be lifted up from the earth, will draw all men unto me."
John12:32

Any gospel, or doctrinal teaching that does not lift up the Name of Jesus Christ is not a sound doctrine. In this Kingdom, it's all about praise.

Although In this book, I will be sharing a few mysteries of praise that provokes the supernatural power of God to come down.

We were told, *"And when they began to sing and to praise, the Lord set ambushments against the children of Ammon, Moab, and mount Seir, which were come against Judah; and they were smitten."*
2chronicle20:22

Praise is an expression of our faith in God. In this book, I will be sharing also how to render praise with understanding. There are a lot of bitter, and wicked people, living a defeated life style. The sincerity of your heart can only be measured in your praise life.

I pray you embrace the mystery of praise in your pursuit of happiness in Jesus Name.

I may never meet you in person-one to one, but may this small book serve its purpose. It is written, *"Great is the Lord, and greatly to be praised in the city of our God, in the mountain of his holiness."* **Psalm 48:1**

"Sing unto God, sing praises to his name: extol him that rideth upon the heavens by his name Jah, and rejoice before him." **Psalm 68:4**

There is power in praise. The psalmist said, *"Make a joyful noise unto the Lord, all the earth: make a loud noise, and rejoice, and sing praise."* **Psalm98:4**

"And when they began to sing and to praise, the Lord set ambushments against the children of Ammon, Moab, and mount Seir, which were come against Judah; and they were smitten." **2chr20:22**

This book is designed to encourage your life. It is a boaster to help you live a victorious life in Christ Jesus. My aim is to help you see the good things which God have done upon your life. There is good news for you. For unless you discover the power of praise, we will be missing out on the blessing of the Lord. Come with me together let's examine what the Holy Ghost is saying about praise in this great book.

Happy Reading!

HIS DESTINY WAS THE CROSS....

HIS PURPOSE WAS LOVE.....

HIS REASON WAS YOU....

"The spirit of a man will sustain his infirmity; but a wounded spirit who can bear?"

Proverb 18:14

"A merry heart doeth good like a medicine: but a broken spirit drieth the bones."

Prover17:22

"In God I will praise his word, in God I have put my trust; I will not fear what flesh can do unto me."

Psalms 56:4

"But thou art holy, O thou that inhabitest the praises of Israel."

Psalm 22:3

"For God is the King of all the earth: sing ye praises with understanding."

Psalm 47:7

ATTITUDE OF PRAISE

Every time you live a praiseful life, you live a victorious life. Every time you live in complaining & murmuring lifestyle, you live a defeated life. Praising God gives us the secured backing of the great God of heaven. Do not live, "a blameful life". Do not look for who to blame for your short coming in life. Rather give God praise, learn how to take responsibility by faith. Do not always say it's somebody's fault and not your fault. To me praise must become a lifestyle, if you must live a victorious life. You cannot win in life without constant praise to God.

There are a lot of miserable men and women out there in the world. Praise must become our daily attitude. David said *"I will bless the Lord at all times: his praise shall continually be in my mouth."*

If you are truly in this kingdom, then you must know how to praise God at all times.

We were told *"Through Him then, let us continually offer up a sacrifice of praise to God, that is, the fruit of lips that give thanks to His name."* **Hebrew13:15**.

"A man shall be satisfied with good by the fruit of his mouth: and the recompence of a man's hands shall be rendered unto him." **Proverb12:14**

The above scripture tells me that praise is not an elective in the kingdom of God. It is a compulsory subject that every kingdom believer must acquaint themselves with. Especially if they want to succeed and win in life. One of my great mentors was questioned one time, *"Have ever had problems? He responded, May it came and I didn't know."*

That is the mystery of praise in display. Praise will convert problems to opportunities in the eye of the "praiser" if I am permitted to use that word.

Praise must be come out of Joy

For anyone to praise God satisfactory, he or she must be joyful. Praise must come out of a joyful heart. *"Whom having not seen, ye love; in whom, though now ye see him not, yet believing, ye rejoice with joy unspeakable and full of glory:"* **1peter1:8**

"...neither be ye sorry; for the joy of the Lord is your strength." **Neh8:10**.

It is this joy that empowers in praise. Especially when it is done well. I see you winning in Jesus mighty Name.

Praise must come out of a merry heart

Have you ever noticed, every time you live a happy life, you succeed in every that you do *"A merry heart doeth good like a medicine: but a broken spirit drieth the bones."* **Proverb17:22**

Why must praise come out of a happy heart?

For unless you think positive, you will not breakthrough in life. Praise is an expression of your faith in God. It confirms the validity of God's input in your affairs. Whenever you praise God you attracts his presence into your life.

"While I live will I praise the Lord: I will sing praises unto my God while I have any being." **Psalm146:2**

Whenever you complain, and murmur, you are living in defeat of the devil. Listen to me, you are controlled by your most dominant thought.

"For as he thinketh in his heart, so is he: Eat and drink, saith he to thee; but his heart is not with thee." **Proverb23:7**

Praise must be done in truth.

God hates empty shout. God hates people who dance only with their lips, and body, but their heart is far from God. We must always draw near to God with our spirit, soul, and body.

"Wherefore the Lord said, Forasmuch as this people draw near me with their mouth, and with their lips do honour me, but have removed their heart far from me, and their fear toward me is taught by the precept of men:" **Isaiah29:13**

"Draw nigh to God, and he will draw nigh to you. Cleanse your hands, ye sinners; and purify your hearts, ye double minded." **James4:8**

Praise must be sweet to our soul

Every time you are in genuine praise dance, you tend to enjoy the entire moment. David one day enjoyed himself in praise until micah, the wife was provoked to jealousy. Praise must be sweet to your soul.

Otherwise you are not in praise. *"My son, eat thou honey, because it is good; and the honeycomb, which is sweet to thy taste: So shall the knowledge of wisdom be unto thy soul: when thou hast found it, then there shall be a reward, and thy expectation shall not be cut off."* **Proverb24:13-14**

Praise must become a lifestyle

We must understand that our praise to God must be a daily thing. It must not be only when we are in search for a miracle, or breakthrough. *"But thou art holy, O thou that inhabitest the praises of Israel."* **Psalm22:3**

Everyone who lives a praiseful live, lives a victorious life. Everyone who live in murmuring and complaint lives a defeated life. As you operate in praise things will open up for you on its accord. I see you breaking through in Jesus mighty Name.

Praise God for His Benefits

Have God been God to you?

God will never be diminished if you chose not to praise Him. In fact you will be living a defeated life if you chose not to give God praise.

"Bless the Lord, O my soul: and all that is within me, bless his holy name.

Bless the Lord, O my soul, and forget not all his benefits:

Who forgiveth all thine iniquities; who healeth all thy diseases;

Who redeemeth thy life from destruction; who crowneth thee with lovingkindness and tender mercies;

Who satisfieth thy mouth with good things; so that thy youth is renewed like the eagle's.

The Lord executeth righteousness and judgment for all that are oppressed."
Psalm103:1-6

THE NATURE OF PRAISE

Praise must be natural. Praise must be sincere. It must come out of us willingly and freely. *"Great is the Lord, and greatly to be praised; and his greatness is unsearchable."* **Psalm 145:3**

"Praise ye the Lord. Praise ye the name of the Lord; praise him, O ye servants of the Lord.

Ye that stand in the house of the Lord, in the courts of the house of our God. Praise the Lord; for the Lord is good: sing praises unto his name; for it is pleasant." **Psalm 135:1-3**

Praising God in ahead of your miracles make the Holy Ghost to focus on your peculiar case. It will cost you nothing to praise God in private or in public. But it will cost you everything in life when you chose not to praise God. That is to steal God's glory.

Here this,

"Give glory to the Lord your God, before he cause darkness, and before your feet stumble upon the dark mountains, and, while ye look for light, he turn it into the shadow of death, and make it gross darkness." **Jer13:16**.

Herold tried to steal the glory and died instantly

"And immediately the angel of the Lord smote him, because he gave not God the glory: and he was eaten of worms, and gave up the ghost." **Acts12:21**

I pray you in corporate praising God always the remain years of your life in Jesus Mighty Name.

CHAPTER 1
THE POWER OF PRAISE

"Who is like unto thee, O Lord, among the gods? who is like thee, glorious in holiness, fearful in praises, doing wonders?" **Exodus15:11**

God is fearful in praise! Every time we pray God sends angelic help, but whenever we praise, God descend from His throne Himself to intervene. If you doubt me ask Paul and Silas (See acts16:25-26).

The children of Israel prayed all night, nothing happened, but when they began to praise, God came down Himself to fight their battles.

"And when they began to sing and to praise, the Lord set ambushments against the children of Ammon, Moab, and mount Seir, which were come against Judah; and they were smitten." **2chr20:22**

The power of praise is hidden in sharing public testimonies. One day God through Apostle Peter healed a man and he jumped up leaping and praising God in public running like a mad man.

"And he leaping up stood, and walked, and entered with them into the temple, walking, and leaping, and praising God. And all the people saw him walking and praising God:" **Acts3:8-9**

Although Worship pulls down the Holy Spirit, it is the power of praise that manifests the supernatural Power of God. It is also the Power of praise that bring us into the presence of the Holy Spirit. Through the power of praise we attracts the healing power, and peace of God that prevails against any obstacle in life. The Bible says that God inhabits in the praises of His people (Psalm 22:3).

In other words, God *"lives in praise."* This means that praise is an alternative channel to manifest His power and presence. It is not just dancing, and shouting. Praise is an old tradition, it is an aged mystery of the kingdom of God that made men like David to prevail in the midst of great impossibility. Praise to God is an expression of our faith in God. It literally ushers us into His Awesome Power & Presence.

"Praising God, and having favour with all the people. And the Lord added to the church daily such as should be saved." **Acts2:47**

Praise and worship is the "gate-way" to enter into His Presence. The psalmist said, *"Enter into his gates with thanksgiving, and into his courts with praise: be thankful unto him, and bless his name"* **(Psalms 100:4)**.

This validates the teaching of Jesus, that His presence will inhabit the gathering of believers who congregate in His name: *"For where two or three are gathered together in my name, there am I in the midst of them"* **(Matthew 18:20)**.

A "gathering in His name" means that Jesus must be the focus, the center of the assemblage. He must be the one preached about, sung about — the one praised and worshiped.

"I will declare thy name unto my brethren, in the midst of the church will I sing praise unto thee" **(Hebrews 2:12)**.

Consequently, Christ's presence, along with His virtue and anointing, is manifested in this type of gathering.

Have you ever noticed when the "gifts of the Spirit" is in operation in a church service?

The Power, and Presence of the anointing of the Holy Spirit usually becomes evident, subsequent to a mere time of worship and praise. Some think that worship is a response after the Holy Spirit moves upon them. However, it's the other way around. God's presence responds when we move upon Him with worship!

Lifting up Jesus Christ through praise and worship invokes the Lord's presence and power to flow in our midst.

What then is Praise?

Praise means *"to commend, to applaud or magnify"*. For the Christian, praise to God is an expression of worship, lifting-up, and glorifying the Lord. It is an expression of humbling ourselves and centering our attention upon the Lord with heart-felt expressions of love, adoration, and thanksgiving.

High praises bring our spirit into a pinnacle of fellowship and intimacy between ourselves and God — it magnifies our awareness of our spiritual union with the most-High God. Praise transports us into the realm of the supernatural and into the power of God.

"Blessed is the people that know the joyful sound: they shall walk, O LORD, in the light of thy countenance" **(Psalms 89:15)**.

There are many actions involved with praise to God — verbal expressions of adoration and thanksgiving, singing, playing instruments, shouting, dancing, lifting or clapping our hands.

But true praise is not "merely" going through these motions. Jesus spoke about the hypocrisy of the pharisees, whose worship was only an outward show and not from the heart.

"This people draweth nigh unto me with their mouth, and honoureth me with their lips; but their heart is far from me" **(Matthew 15:8)**.

Genuine praise to God is a matter of humility and sincere devotion to the Lord from within.

Unpretentious praise and worship pleases the Lord. He delights in the love and devotion of His children. According to the scriptures, the various expressions of praise bring blessing to the Lord.

He eagerly awaits the fragrance of our affections, desiring to manifest His sweet presence and power in our midst.

"...the true worshipers shall worship the Father in spirit and in truth: for the Father seeketh such to worship him" **(John 4:23)**

Praising must become a daily thing that we do.

Although most people only remember to praise God only inside a church service.

However, praising God must become a daily thing. It should be a part of a believer's daily ritual in life. At work, in the car, at home in bed, or anywhere; praise to the Lord brings the refreshing of the Lord's presence, along with His Power and anointing.

"...I will bless the LORD at all times: his praise shall continually be in my mouth." **(Psalms 34:1)**

To me, praising God is an expression of our faith. It manifests positive confession of our expected victories and triumphant in life. It establishes that we believe in God's word.

Praise is a "sacrificial offering," something that we offer to God sacrificially, not just because we feel like it, but because we believe in Him and desire to please Him.

"By him therefore let us offer the sacrifice of praise to God continually, that is, the fruit of our lips giving thanks to his name" **Hebrews 13:15**

Although you may disagree, our praise life affects our health, finances, and our spirit. It affects every part of our life-spirit, soul, and body. On the contrary, anyone who is always joyful, and happy in life, is someone who is immune to sickness and diseases.

The truth is; anyone who complains and never find a reason to praise God is someone vulnerable to sickness and disease.

Every time you are dried up, you attract cancer, sugar diabetes, high-blood pressure etc. *"A merry heart doeth good like a medicine: but a broken spirit drieth the bones."* **Proverb17:22**

"The spirit of a man will sustain his infirmity; but a wounded spirit who can bear?" **Proverb18:22**

"Then he said unto them, Go your way, eat the fat, and drink the sweet, and send portions unto them for whom nothing is prepared: for this day is holy unto our Lord: neither be ye sorry; for the joy of the Lord is your strength." **Neh8:10**.

What are the conditions for Praise?

-A Pure Heart

Praise is a commandment. Therefore we must praise God even when we do not feel like dancing, or shouting in life. In life there are important things that matters; praise is crucial in the kingdom of God.

Often a lot of people are envious and bitter in their heart. Yet they pretend to praise God with their lips. If you do not have a pure heart, you are not qualified to render quality praise to God. We were told,

"Wherefore the Lord said, Forasmuch as this people draw near me with their mouth, and with their lips do honour me, but have removed their heart far from me, and their fear toward me is taught by the precept of men:" **Isaiah29:13**

- A Forgiven Heart

A heart full of negative thoughts, and evil imagination, have no place in God. If you cannot forgive others of their trespasses, you have no right to come before God in praise.

"Therefore if thou bring thy gift to the altar, and there rememberest that thy brother hath ought against thee; Leave there thy gift before the altar, and go thy way; first be reconciled to thy brother, and then come and offer thy gift." **Mathew5:23-24**

"For if ye forgive men their trespasses, your heavenly Father will also forgive you: But if ye forgive not men their trespasses, neither will your Father forgive your trespasses." **Mathew6:14-15**.

We all must embrace the mystery of forgiveness if we must praise God with understanding. I see God ordering your steps as you praise Him sincerely.

Remember…..

"But I say unto you, That whosoever is angry with his brother without a cause shall be in danger of the judgment: and whosoever shall say to his brother, Raca, shall be in danger of the council: but whosoever shall say, Thou fool, shall be in danger of hell fire." **Mathew5:22**

-A Joyful Heart

Joy is all it takes to manifest God the hand of God in your praise. The bible says *"Is any among you afflicted? Let him pray. Is any merry? Let him sing psalms."*

The bible says *"Therefore with joy shall ye draw water out of the wells of salvation."* **Isaiah12:3**

A Joyful heart is a praiseful heart, and a praiseful heart is a heart full of the wonders of God. Until you remove every sorrow in your life you are ready to praise God with understanding.

It is written *"...neither be ye sorry; for the joy of the Lord is your strength."* **Neh8:10**.

I commend you to practice joy in your heart as you praise Him next time and write me to tell me of your testimonies. I bet you God will show Himself strong on your behave.

- A Merry Heart

God does not require much from us to manifest, especially in time of praise and worship. It is written *"A merry heart doeth good like a medicine: but a broken spirit drieth the bones."* **Proverb17:22**.

"The spirit of a man will sustain his infirmity; but a wounded spirit who can bear?" **Proverb18:14**.

The truth is, no miserable man or woman can offer acceptable Praise unto God. Just like I say all the time

"Our past is behind us, that our future is before us and that our yesterday has ended and the best part of our life is yet to be lived."

"The vine is dried up, and the fig tree languisheth; the pomegranate tree, the palm tree also, and the apple tree, even all the trees of the field, are withered: because joy is withered away from the sons of men." **Joel1:12**

Praise is an instrument of deliverance.

Although Paul and Silas prayed, it was their praise that delivered them from the prison. It is written *"And at midnight Paul and Silas prayed, and sang praises unto God: and the prisoners heard them. And suddenly there was a great earthquake, so that the foundations of the prison were shaken: and immediately all the doors were opened, and every one's bands were loosed."* **Acts16:25-26**

I have noticed that so many people only praise God while inside the church. Once they come out of the worship service, they begin to complain about their house rent, car, job, health, and other related family crisis. Hear this; every one of us must remain Praiseful If we desire to testify in life.

"Faithful is he that calleth you, who also will do it." **1theo5:24**

God hates murmuring and complaining.

Praise must be free of murmuring and complaining; Murmuring is a habit developed as a result of negative thinking.

"Neither murmur ye, as some of them also murmured, and were destroyed of the destroyer." **1Cor10:10**

"And when the people complained, it displeased the LORD: and the LORD heard it; and his anger was kindled; and the fire of the LORD burnt among them, and consumed them that were in the uttermost parts of the camp." **Number11:1**

There are plenty reasons for us to praise God. Yet so many of us allow murmuring and complains to take the first place in our lives.

THE BENEFITS OF PRAISE

1.   Praise Place demand on God.

If you have ever prayed for anything without receiving it, try praising God for that particular thing. Every time we praise God we place demand upon God to act immediately in our favor. *"Praise him for his mighty deeds; praise him according to his excellent greatness!"* **Psalm. 150:2**

Here this…..

The Psalmist said, *"And my tongue shall speak of your righteousness and of your praise all the day long."* **Psalm. 35:28**

2.   Praise humbles us.

As long as you remain humble in life, God will lift you in due time. We were told, *"And I, if I be lifted up from the earth, will draw all men unto me."* **John12:32**

"He hath put down the mighty from their seats, and exalted them of low degree." **Luke 1:52**

We are told, *"Humble yourselves therefore under the mighty hand of God, that he may exalt you in due time:"* **1 Peter 5:6**

"It is a good thing to give thanks unto the Lord, and to sing praises unto thy name, O Most High: To shew forth thy lovingkindness in the morning, and thy faithfulness every night." **Psalms 92:1-2**

"I will give you thanks in the great congregation: I will praise you among much people." **Psa. 35:18**

3. Praise overcomes the devil

"Judah, thou art he whom thy brethren shall praise: thy hand shall be in the neck of thine enemies; thy father's children shall bow down before thee." **Genesis 49:8**

"As they began to sing and praise, the Lord set ambushes against the men of Ammon and Moab and Mount Seir who were invading Judah, and they were defeated" **2 Chron. 20:22**

4. Praise conquers complaining and murmuring.

If you have a praise life, you will overcome complaining and murmuring in life.

"Bless the Lord, O my soul, and forget not all his benefits, who forgives all your iniquity, who heals all your diseases, who redeems your life from the pit, who crowns you with steadfast love and mercy." **Psalm. 103:2-4**

Instead of giving glory to the devil by complaining, why don't we give God praise and allow the presence of God to dominate our life.

"By him therefore let us offer the sacrifice of praise to God continually, that is, the fruit of our lips giving thanks to his name." **Heb. 13:15**

5. Praise makes room for God's blessings over our lives.

He will not hold back His goodness, praise opens the gateway of blessing as we come into the Presence of our King.

Chapter 1 - The Omnipotent Power of God

"Enter his gates with thanksgiving, and his courts with praise! Give thanks to him; bless his name!" **Psa. 100:4**

"Blessed be the God and Father of our Lord Jesus Christ, who has blessed us with all spiritual blessings in heavenly places in Christ:" **Eph. 1:3**

6.   Praise invites His presence.

God dwells close to us when we praise Him. He lives there. He looks for it.

"He inhabits the praises of His people." **Psa. 22:3**

"But you are a chosen generation, a royal priesthood, an holy nation, a peculiar people; that you should show forth the praises of him who has called you out of darkness into his marvelous light;" **1 Pet. 2:9**

7.   Our spirits are refreshed and renewed in His presence.

We're strengthened by His peace and refueled by His joy. Through a heart of praise, we realize that God doesn't just change our situations and work through our problems, He changes our hearts. *"In His presence, there is fullness of joy."* **Psalm. 16:11**

"Because your love is better than life, my lips will glorify you. I will praise you as long as I live, and in your name I will lift up my hands." **Psa. 63:3-4**

8. It paves the way for God's power to be displayed, miracles happen.

People's lives are affected and changed. God shakes things up through praise. As Paul and Silas sat in prison, shackled, and chained, they kept right on praising God. And God sent an earthquake that shook the cells and broke the chains. The jailer and all his family came to know Christ that very night.

"About midnight Paul and Silas were praying and singing hymns to God, and the prisoners were listening to them, and suddenly there was a great earthquake, so that the foundations of the prison were shaken. And immediately all the doors were opened, and everyone's bonds were unfastened." **Acts 16:25-26**

Praise is the expression we give to the 'worship' we live.

Chapter 1 - The Omnipotent Power of God

Praise involves more than a shout

1. Praise means total surrender to God

For unless we surrender to God in praise we will be praising ourselves. Praise invites the Holy Spirit on the scene.

2. Praise Is Putting Our Focus on Him

True worship is based on the desire to honor God. It requires a personal revelation of God as found in the Scriptures. Worship is not based on my likes or dislikes. It is not based on my personal preferences or priorities. It is a focus on Him.

3. Praise makes a way for breakthrough

We have to learn to remove our worries, our opinion, our questions and ourselves—so we can worship with appropriate honor. It's letting go. Sometimes, we get in the way of our own experience of genuine worship.

4. Praise is Sacrificial

Praise can be easier when times are good or we have had the big victory. It requires a sacrifice of our own feelings and fears so we can give Him the focus He deserves.

"Through Jesus, therefore, let us continually offer to God a sacrifice of praise—the fruit of lips that openly profess His name." **Hebrews 13:15**

5. We Must Praise God in the Face of Pain & Loss

King David demonstrated what it means to worship in the face of loss and pain. His baby died. He prayed and prayed, but the baby died. I can't imagine the pain that would come from the loss of a child. The loss of loved ones is too great to bear.

Then David got up from the ground. After he had washed, put on lotions and changed his clothes, he went into the house of the LORD and worshiped. 2 Sam 12:20 NIV

Chapter 1 - The Omnipotent Power of God

It is so important that in times of pain and loss, we move toward God rather than 'away' from Him. David showed us that we have to say, *"I feel so much pain, I'm in agony, but I'm going to go toward God because I need Him more now than ever."*

6. Praise Is Celebrating Who God Is and What He Has Done

Have God done any good thing in your life? Then give him the praise with delight, with joy and with love. God will never change because of our action. So, wheather we praise or do not praise God remains God, from now to generation to come forever and ever. Amen.

CHAPTER 2
HINDRANCES TO PRAISE

"Go through, go through the gates; prepare ye the way of the people; cast up, cast up the highway; gather out the stones; lift up a standard for the people." **Isaiah 62:10**

"And the people gave a shout, saying, It is the voice of a god, and not of a man." **Acts 12:22**.

Often some of us praise idols, others, and ourselves thinking that we are praising God. We have to understand one vital key in praise. God is the king of all the earth, therefore we must praise Him with humility.

Because praise belongs to God, we must give it to him with understanding.

"For God is the King of all the earth: sing ye praises with understanding." **Psalms 47:7**

Chapter 1 - The Omnipotent Power of God

"I will praise the name of God with a song, and will magnify him with thanksgiving." **Psalms69:30**

There are a lot of hindrances that stops quality praise unto God.

One great man of God said *"Put down your umbrella of doubt and unbelief and enjoy the latter rain"*....Unbelief, doubt and ignorant are the greatest hindrance to acceptable praise to God. No man can go far in life without giving quality praise to God continually.

"I will bless the Lord at all times: his praise shall continually be in my mouth." **Psalm34:1**

PRIDE

Pride is a hindrance to praise. Every time you operate in pride, you operate in destruction. The bible says *"Pride goeth before destruction, and an haughty spirit before a fall."* **Proverbs16:18**

Pride means stealing God's glory. The rich fool had a heart attack as he continued to confess in pride what he has done, and what he will do.

"And he said, This will I do: I will pull down my barns, and build greater; and there will I bestow all my fruits and my goods. And I will say to my soul, Soul, thou hast much goods laid up for many years; take thine ease, eat, drink, and be merry. But God said unto him, Thou fool, this night thy soul shall be required of thee: then whose shall those things be, which thou hast provided?" **Luke 12:18-20**

Satan was pushed down from heaven because of pride

"For thou hast said in thine heart, I will ascend into heaven, I will exalt my throne above the stars of God: I will sit also upon the mount of the congregation, in the sides of the north: I will ascend above the heights of the clouds; I will be like the most High. Yet thou shalt be brought down to hell, to the sides of the pit." **Isaiah 14:13-15**

Chapter 1 - The Omnipotent Power of God

We are told *"Hear ye, and give ear; be not proud: for the Lord hath spoken. Give glory to the Lord your God, before he cause darkness, and before your feet stumble upon the dark mountains, and, while ye look for light, he turn it into the shadow of death, and make it gross darkness."* **Jer13:15-16**

"And upon a set day Herod, arrayed in royal apparel, sat upon his throne, and made an oration unto them. And the people gave a shout, saying, it is the voice of a god, and not of a man. And immediately the angel of the Lord smote him, because he gave not God the glory: and he was eaten of worms, and gave up the ghost." **Acts12:21-23**

LIVING IN BITTERNESS

Every time you live in bitterness you cannot render quality praise to God. Looking diligently lest any man fail of the grace of God; lest any root of bitterness springing up trouble you, and thereby many be defiled.

STEALING GOD'S GLORY

"Give glory to the LORD your God, before he cause darkness, and before your feet stumble upon the dark mountains, and, while ye look for light, he turn it into the shadow of death, and make it gross darkness." **Jer13:16**

"I am the LORD: that is my name: and my glory will I not give to another, neither my praise to graven images." **Isaiah42:8**

FORGETFULNESS

Never forget like you have forgot what God has done upon your life.

"Then beware lest thou forget the LORD, which brought thee forth out of the land of Egypt, from the house of bondage." **Deut6:12**

David said *"To the end that my glory may sing praise to thee, and not be silent. O LORD my God, I will give thanks unto thee forever."* **Psalms30:12**

Chapter 1 - The Omnipotent Power of God

COVETOUSNESS

God will never be reduced. Even when you reduce God in your own eyes, He is still the great God. Often we covet and refuse to appreciate what God has done upon our life. *"But godliness with contentment is great gain."* **1tim6:6**

For we brought nothing into this world, and it is certain we can carry nothing out. And having food and raiment let us be therewith content. Jesus said in Luke12:15 And he said unto them, Take heed, and beware of covetousness: for a man's life consisteth not in the abundance of the things which he possesseth.

SERVING OTHER GODS

Admiring and giving priority to other mortals and material things, worshiping idols, sacrificing and serving other image gods is a sin and a hindrance in your praise. Until you begin to serve the most high God, you will have no place in the kingdom of God.

Have you not heard, ye shall serve the Lord your God and he will bless your bread and your water, take away sickness and your young ones will not die before their time? Plus the numbers of your days he will fulfil. (See exodus23;25-26 paraphrase)

The bible says, in Deut28:47-48, Because thou servedst not the LORD thy God with joyfulness, and with gladness of heart, for the abundance of all things; Therefore shalt thou serve thine enemies which the LORD shall send against thee, in hunger, and in thirst, and in nakedness, and in want of all things: and he shall put a yoke of iron upon thy neck, until he have destroyed thee.

Chapter 2 - The Benefits of the Power of God

Four different kinds of praise

1) Praise for Deliverance:

It is written *"But when they began to sing praise an angel of God responded for their deliverance. And at midnight Paul and Silas prayed, and sang praises unto God: and the prisoners heard them. And suddenly there was a great earthquake, so that the foundations of the prison were shaken: and immediately all the doors were opened, and every one's bands were loosed."*
Acts16:25-26

2) Praise for Vengeance:

"Let the high praises of God be in their mouth, and a two-edged sword in their hand; To execute vengeance upon the heathen, and punishments upon the people."
Psalms149:6

O Lord God, to whom vengeance belongeth; O God, to whom vengeance belongeth, shew thyself.

3) Praise for Victory:

As a believer victory is our inheritance. It is written, we are the head and not the tail. Therefore victory must be your portion at every battle, it must be your lot at all obstacle. It must also be your winning ticket at any challenge in your life. Joshua 6:16

And it came to pass at the seventh time, when the priests blew with the trumpets, Joshua said unto the people, Shout; for the LORD hath given you the city.

Joshua 6:20 So the people shouted when the priests blew with the trumpets: and it came to pass, when the people heard the sound of the trumpet, and the people shouted with a great shout, that the wall fell down flat, so that the people went up into the city, every man straight before him, and they took the city.

4) Praise for Judgment:

God is the judge of all the earth. Abraham said concerning God in That be far from thee to do after this manner, to slay the righteous with the wicked: and that the righteous should be as the wicked, that be far from thee: Shall not the Judge of all the earth do right? Genesis18:25.

Chapter 2 - The Benefits of the Power of God

The most High God executes judgment upon the heathen and punishment upon the wicked and unrighteous people.

"To execute upon them the judgment written: this honour have all his saints. Praise ye the LORD." **Psalms 149:9**

"And when they began to sing and to praise, the LORD set ambushments against the children of Ammon, Moab, and mount Seir, which were come against Judah; and they were smitten." **2Chr20:22**

"And when Jehoshaphat and his people came to take away the spoil of them, they found among them in abundance both riches with the dead bodies, and precious jewels, which they stripped off for themselves, more than they could carry away: and they were three days in gathering of the spoil, it was so much." **2chr20:25**

"By him therefore let us offer the sacrifice of praise to God continually, that is, the fruit of our lips giving thanks to his name." **Hebrew13:15**

THE NATURE OF PRAISE

Praise, according to the Scriptures, is an act of our will that flows out of an awe and reverence for our Creator. Praise gives glory to God and opens us up to a deeper union with Him. It turns our attention off of our problems and on the nature and character of God Himself.

As we focus our minds on God and proclaim His goodness, we reflect His glory back to Him. The results can fill you with peace and contentment (Isaiah 26:3) and transform your outlook on life.

REASONS TO PRAISE GOD

Very simply, we praise God because He is worthy of our praise (1 Chron. 16:25; Rev. 5:11-14). He is the Alpha and Omega, the Beginning and the End, the King of kings and Lord of lords. He is our Creator, Provider, Healer, Redeemer, Judge, Defender and much more.

Chapter 2 - The Benefits of the Power of God

Another foundational reason to praise God is simple obedience. The Bible says God is a "jealous" God who demands and desires our praise. *"You shall have no other gods before Me,"* says the first commandment (Deut. 6:7). As the psalmist said, *"Let everything that has breath praise the Lord"* (Psalm 150:6).

As we praise God, we will discover incredible benefits for our lives. That's because human beings were created by God to praise Him (Isa. 43:7, Matt. 21:16). Due to man's original sin, however, this relationship was disrupted. Praising God helps restore us to that right relationship, for God actually dwells in the praises of His people (Psalm 22:3). As we draw near to the Father in praise, He draws near to us (James 4:8).

Praise is also our ultimate destiny. When the Lord Jesus Christ returns again to earth, all creation -- including prideful mankind -- will recognize His glory and praise Him (Phil. 2:9-11).

PRAISE FOR PROTECTION

God also gives us assurances of additional blessings as we praise Him. When we praise God, He honors us as His children, and provides His loving protection (2 Sam. 22:47-51).

Failure to praise God, however, leaves us out of fellowship with God and out of His divine protection (1 Samuel 2:27-32).

Our praise can also serve as a powerful witness to those who do not know the Lord (1 Peter 2:9).

Also, God can work miraculously through our praises. The ancient walls of Jericho came crashing down, giving victory to God's people, as a result of shouts of praise (Joshua 6:1-21).

The prison doors shook open when Paul and Silas praised God (Acts 16:25-26).

Chapter 2 - The Benefits of the Power of God

PRAISE FOR MIRACLE

Whenever you are Godfull, if I am permitted to use that word, you will be praiseful, and whenever you are praiseful, you will be full of, wonders. Praise is the key into the supernatural.

LIVING A LIFE OF PRAISE

It is vitally important to live in an attitude of praise toward God. But what can you do if you are having difficulty maintaining a life filled with praise?

1.   Commit your life to Christ.

A committed life is a save worthy to be saved. God will never save uncommitted people. We must be absolutely sure that we have placed our life completely-through faith in Jesus Christ as Lord and Savior. The Bible says that "if you confess with your mouth Jesus as Lord, and believe in your heart that God raised Him from the dead, you shall be saved" (Romans. 10:9).

2. Confess and repent.

A pure heart is a heart full of praise. Sin as a hindrance must be confessed unto God. *"Then Peter said unto them, Repent, and be baptized every one of you in the name of Jesus Christ for the remission of sins, and ye shall receive the gift of the Holy Ghost."* Acts 2:38

3. Praise God regardless of prevailing obstacles:

There is never a better time to praise God. In good times and into trial times, we must embrace praise to God as a lifestyle. Despite our present challenges in life, it is important to offer praise to God.

4. Join together with other believers.

Sharing your struggles with another brother or sister in Christ is not only good idea (Ecc. 4:9-10), it is commanded (James 5:16). Uniting with other believers in regular worship is also a key to being able to praise God (Heb. 10:24-25).

Chapter 2 - The Benefits of the Power of God

ALWAYS PRAY AND PRAISE

Are you living a life filled with praise for God? If not, take a few moments to examine your life and your relationship with Jesus. If you have not made Him Lord of your life, start there. Then, confess any known sin and receive His forgiveness. Ask Him to renew you and refresh your spirit.

"Lord, You have made me and You love me. Forgive me for failing to give You the praise which You deserve. I confess my need of You in all things. I desire to walk in joy and praise. Release me now into a deeper understanding of who You are, so that I may truly praise You. I ask all this in Jesus' name. Amen."

THE POWER OF PRAISE

"Sing to the Lord, all the earth; Proclaim good tidings of His salvation from day to day. Tell of His glory among the nations, His wonderful deeds among all the peoples. For great is the Lord, and greatly to be praised; He also is to be feared above all gods" (1 Chron. 16:23-25)

Benefits of Praise

Unlimited insight:

None of us is permitted to obtain divine insight unless we position ourselves before Him through our praise. It is written *"I will praise the name of God with a song, and will magnify him with thanksgiving."* **Psalms 69:30**

Divine Presence:

"Thou wilt shew me the path of life: in thy presence is fulness of joy; at thy right hand there are pleasures for evermore." Praising God continually provokes divine presence. Praising God, and having favour with all the people. And the Lord added to the church daily such as should be saved."

Divine Ideas:

It is written *"But there is a spirit in man: and the inspiration of the Almighty giveth them understanding."* **Job 32:8**.

As long as you are bitter in the inside, you will not hear from God. If you must access divine ideas, we must embrace praise as a lifestyle.

Chapter 2 - The Benefits of the Power of God

Ever-ending Progress:

"But the path of the just is as the shining light, that shineth more and more unto the perfect day." Proverb4:18. *If you must make headline news, you must continually be in praise with God and men. It is written "I will bless the Lord at all times: his praise shall continually be in my mouth."* **Psalms34:4.**

Unstoppable access and supply into the supernatural:

If you we must access unending supply of the supernatural acts of God, we must embrace praising God, as a lifestyle. Nothing about us, is permitted to multiply unless we praise our way into it.

CONCLUSION

"Let everything that has breath praise the Lord. Praise the Lord." **Pslams150:6**

"Therefore if any man be in Christ, he is a new creature: old things are passed away; behold, all things are become new." **2cor5:17**

What must I do to determine my divine visitation?

To determine divine visitation you must be born again. The word says as many as received him, to them gave He power to become the sons of God. Even to them that believe on his name.

To qualify for divine visitation do the following sincerely;

1) Acknowledge that you are a sinner and that He died for you. **Rom3:23**.

2) Repent of your sins. **Acts 3:19, Luke13:5, 2Peter3:9**

Chapter 2 - The Benefits of the Power of God

3) Believe in your heart that Jesus died for your sin. **Romans10:10**

4) Confess Jesus as the Lord over your life. **Romans10:10, Acts2:21**

Now repeat this Prayer after me

      Say Lord Jesus, I accept you today, as my Lord and my savior, forgive me of my sins wash me with your blood. Right now, I believe, I am sanctified, I am save, I am free, I am free from the Power of sin to serve the Lord Jesus. Thank you Lord for saving me.

      I am inviting you to come and worship with me every Wednesday, Friday, Saturdays, and Sundays.

MIRACLE OF GOD MINISTRIES

343 Sanford Avenue, Newark New Jersey 07106

Website: www.fnabaziehealingministries.org

Below is our worship service schedule;

Worship Service

Wednesdays: 7:00pm-9:00pm –Bible study

Fridays: 6:00pm-9:00pm Prophetic breakthrough service

Saturdays: 10:45am-12:45pm Financial Empowerment

Sundays: 10:45am-12:45pm Prophetic healing & Deliverance service

Chapter 2 - The Benefits of the Power of God

WISDOM KEYS

Every Productive Society is a society heading to the top

Millions of Nigerians run away from Nigeria, very few Nigerians stay in Nigeria.

My decision to return Nigeria is the will of God for my life

My short coming in America after 18 years, trained me to be wise, to think, reflect and reason appropriately.

If you train your mind to reason it will train your hands to earn money.

It is absurd to use the money of the heathen to build the kingdom of the living God.

Every Ministry reveals its agenda and goal either at the beginning or at the end. Be careful of your life it is your first Ministry.

The average American mind is conditioned for a continual quest to get new things and (discard the former) and throw away old things.

When I considered well, my BMW jeep became my initial deposit for the work of the ministry in Nigeria

Everyone is waiting for you to change your mind until you change your thinking nothing changes around you.

Multiple academic degrees in other discipline gave me the chance to think, reflect and reason

What so everyone are thinking and reflecting at the moment reveals you to the time and the now factor

All events and intents are the product of precise thought processes, accurate reason every event is designed for a designated timeline

Wisdom is your ability to think, to create and invent. If you can think wise enough you will come out of penury

The distance between you and success is your creative ability to think reason and reflect accurate.

Chapter 2 - The Benefits of the Power of God

Success is the result of hard work, commitment resolve and determination learning from past mistakes and failing.

If you organize your mind you have organized your life and destiny.

There is a thin line between success and failure. If you look above and beyond you are on your way to success.

Wealth is your ability to think, power is your ability to reason and success is your ability to be informed.

If you can make use of your mind by thinking and reasoning God will make use of your life and destiny.

Think and Be Great

Reflect, Reason, think and be great

Famous people are born of woman

That you will make it is your intention; that you will survive is your resolve, that you will succeed with changes is your determination, personal efforts and hard work.

No man was born a failure. Lack of vision is the end product of failure.

Working with mental patients encourages and aspire me to be a productive observant and dedicated to my assignment.

Successful people are not magicians, it is the will power combined with hard work, and determination and a resolve to succeed that make them succeed.

In the unequivocal state of the mind, intention is not a location or a position it is the state of the mind.

So many people think that they think. The mind is used to think reflect and reason. You will remain blind with your eye open until you can see with your mind by thinking.

There is no favoritism in accurate and precise calculation

Chapter 2 - The Benefits of the Power of God

Although knowledge is power, information is the key and gateway to a great future.

It will take the hand of God to move the hand of man.

With the backing of the great wise God, nothing will disconnect you from your inheritance.

As long as you have wisdom and understanding of God, Satan and evil cannot manipulate your life and destiny.

You have come this far by yourself judgment and decision you have made in the past, now lean and listen to God for another dimension of greatness.

Great people are common people it is extra ordinary effort and the price of sacrifice that produces greatness.

As a mental direct care worker I saw a great pastor and a motivational speaker within myself.

Menial job does not reduce your self-worth, until you resolve to achieve greatness see greatness in all you do; you will never count in your community

The principle of Jesus will solve your gambling and addiction problems

The man of Jesus will lead you into heaven,

Everyone have their self-appraisal and what they think about you. Until you discover yourself other opinion about you will alter the real you.

Supervisors and directors are just a position in the chain of command in a work place. Never allow your supervisor hierarchy to alter your opinion about yourself.

Everyone can come out of debt if they make up their mind.

That I am not a decision maker at work does not diminish my contribution to my world.

Although it appears like it was a poor decision to accept a direct care employment at a psychiatric hospital as I reflect of my nine years of experience, it became apparent that I have learnt and experienced enough for my next assignment.

Self-encouragement and determination is a resolve of the heart.

Chapter 3 - Prayer of Salvation

If you are determined to make a difference, and do the things that make a difference you will eventually make a difference.

Good things do not come easy

Short cuts will cut your life short.

Those who look ahead move ahead.

Life is all about making an impact. In your life time strive to make an impact in your community.

Make friends and connect with people who are moving ahead of you in life.

If you can look around well you have come a long way in your life, made a lot of difference and realized a lot of success in life.

If you are my old friend, hurry up to reach out to me before I become a stranger to you.

Everything I am blessed with inspirations from God, that change my definition and interpretation of the world around me.

I thought I was stagnant and lonely until I looked around and noticed my children running around and my wife cooking.

At 40 I resigned my Job to seek the Lord forever.

My ministry took a drastic rise to the top when the wisdom of God visited me with knowledge and understanding.

You will be a better person if you understand the characteristics of your personality – your mood swings attitudes and habits.

It is the seed of love you sow into the heart of a child and a woman that you reap in due time.

Love is not selfish, love share everything including the concealed secrets of the mind.

As long as you have a prayer life and a bible; you will never feel lonely, rejected and idle in the race of life.

When good friends disconnect from you, let them go, they might have seen something new in a different direction.

Confidence in yourself and in God is the only way to bring you out of captivity

Never train a child to waste his/her time.

The mind is the greatest assets of a great future.

Chapter 3 - Prayer of Salvation

You walk by common sense run by principles and fly by instruction.

Those who fly in flight of life fly alone.

Up in the air you are alone. No one can toll you accept the compass of knowledge and information

I have seen a tolling vehicle I have seen a tolling ship I have never seen a tolling airplane.

I exercise my judgment and make a decision every minute of the day.

Decisions are crucial, critical and vital with reference to your future.

So many people wish for a great future. You can only work towards a great future.

Your celebrity status began when you discovered your talent. What are you good at? Work at it with all commitment.

Prayers will sustain you but the wisdom of God will prosper you.

When I met Oyedepo, his teachings changed my perspective, but when I met Ibiyeomie; His teaching changed my perception.

I will be successful in ministry if only I concentrate and focus my energy in the work of the ministry.

It took the late Dr. Vincent Pearle Norman's book to open my mind towards kingdom success.

CHAPTER 3
PRAYER OF SALVATION

"Neither is there salvation in any other: for there is none other name under heaven given among men, whereby we must be saved." **Acts4:12**

The first decision is to be born again. A decision for Christ.

To be saved we must be born again!

The word says as many as received him, to them gave He power to become the sons of God. Even to them that believe on his name.

To qualify for divine visitation do the following sincerely,

1) Acknowledge that you are a sinner and that He died for you. **Rom3:23.**

2) Repent of your sins. **Acts 3:19, Luke13:5, 2Peter3:9**

3) Believe in your heart that Jesus died for your sin. **Romans10:10**

4) Confess Jesus as the Lord over your life. **Romans10:10, Acts2:21**

Now repeat this Prayer after me

Say Lord Jesus, I accept you today, as my Lord and my savior, forgive me of my sins wash me with your blood. Right now, I believe, I am sanctified, I am save, I am free, I am free from the Power of sin to serve the Lord Jesus. Thank you Lord for saving me. Amen.

I adjure you to watch the Spirit of God bear witness with your Spirit confirming His word with signs following. The word says The Spirit itself beareth witness with our spirit, that we are the children of God.

Chapter 3 - Prayer of Salvation

MIRACLE CARE OUTREACH

"...But that the members should have the same care one for another" **1cor12:25**

We are all members of the body of Christ. Jesus commanded us to love our neighbor as ourselves. This includes caring for one another as a member of one body. True love is expressed in caring and giving. The word says for God so Love He gave….

Reach out to someone in need of Jesus, help someone in crisis find Christ. Look out and prove your love to Jesus by caring and inviting your friends and associates to find Jesus the Healer.

Invite your friends to our Home Care Cell Fellowship (Miracle chapel Intl Satellite fellowship) In the USA at 33 Schley Street Newark New Jersey 07112.

If you are in Nigeria—**MIRACLE OF GOD MINISTRIES**

A.K.A"MIRACLE CHAPEL INTL"
Mpama –Egbu-Owerri Imo state Nigeria.

(Home Care Cell fellowship Group). We meet every Tuesday at 6:00pm-7:00pm.

LIFE IS NOT ALL ABOUT DURATION BUT ITS ALL ABOUT DONATION

What does the above statement mean?....

"Life consists not in accumulation of material wealth.." **Luke 12:15.**

"But it's all about liberality....meaning- what you can give and share with others." **Proverb 11:25.**

When you live for others--You live forever- because you out live your generation by the legacy you live behind after you depart into glory to be with the Lord. But when you live to yourself - you are reduced to self—you are easily forgotten when you die and depart in glory.

Permit me to admonish you today to live your life to be a blessing to a soul connected to you today.

Chapter 4 - About the Author

I want you to know that so many souls are connected and looking up to you, and through you so many souls will be saved and rescued from destruction. Will you disciple someone today to find Jesus Christ?

"As a genuine Christian; it is your duty to evangelize Jesus Christ to all you meet on your way. Jesus is still in the healing business-Jesus is still doing miracles from time of old to now.

Therefore tell someone about Jesus Christ today, disciple and bring them to Church."

John 1:45 Philip findeth Nathanael....

Please to prove the sincerity of your love for God today; please become a soul winner. The dignity of your Christianity is hidden in your boldness to proclaim and evangelize Jesus Christ to all you meet on your way.

There is a question mark on the integrity of your Christianity until you become a life soul winner. Invite someone to join us worship the Lord Jesus this coming Sunday.

MIRACLE OF GOD MINISTRIES

PILLARS OF THE COMMISSION

We Believe Preach and Practice the following,

1) We believe and preach Salvation to every living human being

2) We believe and preach Repentance and forgiveness of sins

3) We believe and preach the baptism of the Holy Spirit and Spiritual gifts

4) We believe and teach the Prosperity

5) We believe and preach Divine Healing and Miracles (Signs & Wonder)

6) We believe and preach Faith

7) We believe and Proclaim the Power of God (Supernatural)

8) We believe and Proclaim Praise & Worship to God

9) We believe and preach Wisdom

10) We believe and preach Holiness (Consecration)

11) We believe and preach Vision

12) We believe and teach the Word of God

13) We believe and teach Success

14) We believe and practice Prayer

15) We believe and teach Deliverance

This 15 stones form the Pillars of Our Commission.

Become part of this church family and follow this great move of God.

MY HEART FELT PRAYER FOR YOU

It is my vision to spread the word of God in print. It is also my vision for you to come to the knowledge of Christ Jesus.

I love desire for you to meet God through one of our books, video's, or other related materials. I will love to hear of your testimonies and encounter with the Lord Jesus. I love for you to take a few minutes and write me a note below.

REV FRANKLIN N ABAZIE

MIRACLE OF GOD MINISTRIES

33 SCHLEY STREET NEARK NEW JERSEY 07112

OR AT MY WORSHIP ADDRESS AT

MIRACLE OF GOD MINISTRIES

343 SANFORD AVENUE

NEWARK NEW JERSEY 07106

Now let me Pray for you:

Father I thank you for hearing me always. Even now oh God, let us experience you free Spirit of power, sound mind and wisdom. In Jesus Mighty Name.

Amen

I like for you to believe in God, for there is nothing God cannot do for us.

"Therefore I say unto you, What things soever ye desire, when ye pray, believe that ye receive them, and ye shall have them." **Mark 11:24**

I love for you to also develop a prayer life, for there is power in prayer.

"And he spake a parable unto them to this end, that men ought always to pray, and not to faint;" **Luke 18:1**

"And the prayer of faith shall save the sick, and the Lord shall raise him up; and if he have committed sins, they shall be forgiven him. Confess your faults one to another, and pray one for another, that ye may be healed. The effectual fervent prayer of a righteous man availeth much." **James 5:15-16**

"Go ye therefore, and teach all nations, baptizing them in the name of the Father, and of the Son, and of the Holy Ghost:" **Mathew28:18**

Finally we must win souls for Jesus. We are admonished *"The fruit of the righteous is a tree of life; and he that winneth souls is wise."* May you win more souls for the kingdom of God.

Amen

CHAPTER 4
ABOUT THE AUTHOR

Rev Franklin N Abazie is the founding and Presiding Pastor of Miracle of God Ministries with headquarters in Newark, New Jersey USA and a branch church in Owerri- Imo State Nigeria. He is following the footsteps of one of his mentors, Oral Roberts (Healing Evangelist) of the blessed memory.

The Lord passed Oral Roberts healing mantle two days before he went to be with the Lord at age 91 into the hand of healing evangelist-Rev Franklin N Abazie in a vision.

In all his services the Power and Presence of God is present to heal all in his audience. He is an ordained man of God with a Healing Ministry reviving the healing and miracle ministry of Jesus Christ of Nazareth.

Pastor Franklin N Abazie, is called by God with a unique mandate:

"THE MOMENT IS DUE TO IMPACT YOUR WORLD THROUGH THE REVIVAL OF THE HEALING & MIRACLE MINISTRY OF JESUS CHRIST OF NAZARETH.

I AM SENDING YOU TO RESTORE HEALTH UNTO THEE AND I WILL HEAL THEE OF THY WOUNDS. SAID THE LORD OF HOST"

He is a gifted ardent Teacher of the word of God who operates also in the office of a Prophet, generating and attracting undeniable signs & wonders, special miracles and healings, with apostolic fireworks of the Holy Ghost.

He is the founding and presiding senior Pastor of this fast growing Healing ministry.

He has written over 86 inspirational, healing and transforming books covering almost all aspect of divine healing and life. He is happily married and blessed with children.

BOOKS BY REV FRANKLIN N ABAZIE

1) Commanding Abundance
2) The outcome of faith
3) Understanding the secret of prevailing prayers
4) Understanding the secret of the man God uses
5) Activating my due Season
6) Overcoming Divine Verdicts
7) The Outcome of Divine Wisdom
8) Understanding God's Restoration Mandate
9) Walking in the Victory and Authority of the truth
10) Gods Covenant Exemption
11) Destiny Restoration Pillars
12) Provoking Acceptable Praise
13) Understanding Divine Judgment
14) Activating Angelic Re-enforcement
15) Provoking Un-Merited Favor
16) The Benefits of the Speaking faith
17) Understanding Divine Arrangement

18) Understanding Divine Healing
19) The Mystery of Endurance
20) Obeying Divine Instructions
21) Understanding the Voice of God
22) Never give up on Hope
23) The prevailing Power of faith
24) Understanding Divine Prosperity
25) The Reward of Prayer
26) Covenant Keys to Answered Prayers
27) Activating the Forces of Vengeance
28) Put your faith to work
29) Where is your trust?
30) The Audacity of the Blood of Jesus
31) Redeeming Your Days
32) The force of Vision
33) Breaking the shackles of Family Curses
34) Wisdom for Marriage Stability
35) The winners Faith
36) The Prayer solution
37) The power of Prayer
38) Prayer strategy
39) The prayer that works
40) Walking in Forgiveness
41) The power of the grace of God

42) The power of Persistence
43) Overcoming Divine verdicts
44) The prevailing power of the blood of Jesus
45) The benefit of the speaking faith.
46) Fearless faith
47) Redeeming Your Days.
48) The Supernatural Power of Prophecy
49) The companionship of the Holy Spirit
50) Understanding Divine Judgement
51) Understanding Divine Prosperity
52) Dominating Controlling Forces
53) The winners Faith
54) Destiny Restoration Pillars
55) Developing Spiritual Muscles
56) Inexplicable faith
57) The lifestyle of Prayer
58) Developing a positive attitude in life.
59) The mystery of Divine supply
60) Encounter with God's Power
61) Walking in love
62) Praying in the Spirit
63) How to provoke your testimony

64) Walking in the reality of the Anointing
65) The reality of new birth
66) The price of freedom
67) The Supernatural power of faith
68) The intellectual components of Redemption
69) Overcoming Fear
70) Overcoming Prevailing Challenges
71) The Power of the Grace of God
72) My life & Ministry
73) The Mystery of Praise

MIRACLE OF GOD MINISTRIES

NIGERIA CRUSADE 2012

MIRACLE OF GOD MINISTRIES
NIGERIA CRUSADE 2012

MIRACLE OF GOD MINISTRIES

NIGERIA CRUSADE

2012

MIRACLE OF GOD MINISTRIES

NIGERIA CRUSADE

2012

www.ingramcontent.com/pod-product-compliance
Lightning Source LLC
Chambersburg PA
CBHW020125130526
44591CB00032B/526